C000161951

DON'T PANIC

YOU'RE ONLY

40!

summersdale

DON'T PANIC, YOU'RE ONLY 40!

An Hachette UK Company
www.hachette.co.uk

Summersdale Publishers Ltd
Part of Octopus Publishing Group Limited
Carmelite House
50 Victoria Embankment
LONDON
EC4Y 0DZ

www.summersdale.com

Printed and bound in the Czech Republic

ISBN: 978-1-78685-293-9

Substantial discounts on bulk quantities of Summersdale books are available to corporations, professional associations and other organisations. For details contact general enquiries: telephone: +44 (0) 1243 771107 or email: enquiries@summersdale.com.

TO........................

FROM.....................

CONTENTS

ANOTHER YEAR

OLDER

—

WE DON'T UNDERSTAND
LIFE ANY BETTER AT 40
THAN AT 20, BUT WE
KNOW IT AND ADMIT IT.

—

JULES RENARD

LIKE MANY
WOMEN
MY AGE,
I AM 28
YEARS OLD.

MARY SCHMICH

THE LOVELY THING
ABOUT BEING 40 IS THAT
YOU CAN APPRECIATE
25-YEAR-OLD MEN MORE.

Colleen McCullough

LIFE BEGINS AT 40 –
BUT SO DO FALLEN
ARCHES, RHEUMATISM,
FAULTY EYESIGHT,

AND THE TENDENCY TO
TELL A STORY TO THE
SAME PERSON, THREE
OR FOUR TIMES.

Helen Rowland

YOU'RE NOT 40 –
YOU'RE 18 WITH
22 YEARS'
EXPERIENCE.

Anonymous

IT TAKES
A LONG TIME
TO BECOME YOUNG.

Pablo Picasso

I'M 40 AND I
FEEL GREAT. FEEL
FOR YOURSELF!

Anonymous

LIFE BEGINS
AT 40.

W. B. PITKIN

THIS WINE IS 40 YEARS OLD.

IT CERTAINLY DOESN'T SHOW ITS AGE.

Cicero

—

WHEN I PASSED 40
I DROPPED PRETENCE,
'CAUSE MEN LIKE
WOMEN WHO
GOT SOME SENSE.

—

MAYA ANGELOU

FORTY ISN'T OLD, IF YOU'RE A TREE.

Anonymous

AS A GRADUATE
OF THE ZSA ZSA GABOR
SCHOOL OF CREATIVE
MATHEMATICS,
I HONESTLY DO NOT
KNOW HOW OLD I AM.

Erma Bombeck

AT 20 YEARS
OF AGE, THE
WILL REIGNS. AT
30, THE WIT.
AND AT 40,
THE JUDGEMENT.

Benjamin Franklin

AT 15, MY MIND WAS
BENT ON LEARNING.
AT 30, I STOOD FIRM.

AT 40, I HAD
NO DOUBTS.

Confucius

JUST WHAT I
ALWAYS
WANTED

A HUG IS
THE PERFECT GIFT;
ONE SIZE FITS ALL,
AND NOBODY MINDS
IF YOU EXCHANGE IT.

Anonymous

WHY IS A BIRTHDAY CAKE
THE ONLY FOOD YOU CAN
BLOW ON AND SPIT ON
AND EVERYBODY RUSHES
TO GET A PIECE?

Bobby Kelton

FOR MY 40TH I ASKED
HER FOR A DIRTY
WEEKEND. SHE GAVE ME
A TRIP TO THE BRITISH
BOG SNORKELLING
CHAMPIONSHIPS.

ANONYMOUS

THE LORD LOVETH A CHEERFUL GIVER.

HE ALSO ACCEPTETH FROM A GROUCH.

Catherine Hall

—

A WISE LOVER VALUES
NOT SO MUCH THE GIFT
OF THE LOVER AS THE
LOVE OF THE GIVER.

—

THOMAS À KEMPIS

YOUTH IS THE GIFT OF NATURE, BUT AGE IS A WORK OF ART.

Garson Kanin

A TRUE FRIEND REMEMBERS YOUR BIRTHDAY BUT NOT YOUR AGE.

Anonymous

BIRTHDAYS ARE GOOD
FOR YOU. STATISTICS
SHOW THAT THE PEOPLE
WHO HAVE THE MOST
LIVE THE LONGEST.

Larry Lorenzoni

I DO WISH I COULD TELL YOU MY AGE BUT IT'S IMPOSSIBLE.

IT KEEPS CHANGING ALL THE TIME.

Greer Garson

BIRTHDAYS ARE
NATURE'S WAY
OF TELLING
US TO EAT
MORE CAKE.

Anonymous

THE BEST
BIRTHDAYS ARE
ALL THOSE THAT
HAVEN'T ARRIVED YET.

Robert Orben

WE KNOW WE'RE GETTING
OLD WHEN THE ONLY
THING WE WANT FOR
OUR BIRTHDAY IS NOT
TO BE REMINDED OF IT.

ANONYMOUS

I HAVE EVERYTHING

I HAD 20

YEARS AGO,

ONLY IT'S ALL A

LITTLE BIT LOWER.

GYPSY ROSE LEE

WHEN IT COMES TO STAYING YOUNG,

A MIND-LIFT BEATS A FACE-LIFT ANY DAY.

Marty Bucella

GRIN AND BEAR IT

—

GETTING OLD IS A BIT
LIKE GETTING DRUNK;
EVERYONE ELSE
LOOKS BRILLIANT.

—

BILLY CONNOLLY

THE FIRST 40 YEARS OF
LIFE GIVE US THE TEXT;
THE NEXT 30 SUPPLY THE
COMMENTARY ON IT.

Arthur Schopenhauer

WE TURN NOT **OLDER** WITH YEARS, BUT NEWER EVERY DAY.

EMILY DICKINSON

AGE IS AN ISSUE OF MIND OVER MATTER.

IF YOU DON'T MIND, IT DOESN'T MATTER.

Anonymous

'AGE' IS THE
ACCEPTANCE OF
A TERM OF YEARS.
BUT MATURITY IS THE
GLORY OF YEARS.

Martha Graham

YOUTH IS
A CIRCUMSTANCE YOU
CAN'T DO ANYTHING
ABOUT. THE TRICK
IS TO GROW UP
WITHOUT GETTING OLD.

Frank Lloyd Wright

YOU CAN'T TURN
BACK THE CLOCK,
BUT YOU CAN WIND
IT UP AGAIN.

Bonnie Prudden

I KNEW I WAS GOING
BALD WHEN IT WAS
TAKING ME LONGER
AND LONGER TO
WASH MY FACE.

HARRY HILL

I BELIEVE
IN LOYALTY.
WHEN A
WOMAN
REACHES A
CERTAIN AGE

SHE LIKES, SHE SHOULD STICK WITH IT.

Eva Gabor

AGE IS SOMETHING THAT DOESN'T MATTER, UNLESS YOU ARE A CHEESE.

Billie Burke

—

YOU CAN'T HELP
GETTING OLDER,
BUT YOU DON'T
HAVE TO GET OLD.

—

GEORGE BURNS

I WANT TO LIVE TO
BE 80 SO I CAN
P*SS MORE PEOPLE OFF.

Charles Bukowski

TIME HAS A
WONDERFUL
WAY OF
WEEDING OUT
THE TRIVIAL.

Richard Ben Sapir

YOUTH IS A WONDERFUL THING.

WHAT A CRIME TO WASTE IT ON CHILDREN.

George Bernard Shaw

PUSHING 40?
SHE'S HANGING ON
FOR DEAR LIFE.

IVY COMPTON-BURNETT

**AGEING IS
NOT 'LOST YOUTH'
BUT A NEW STAGE
OF OPPORTUNITY
AND STRENGTH.**

Betty Friedan

WHEN IT COMES TO
AGE WE'RE ALL IN THE
SAME BOAT, ONLY SOME
OF US HAVE BEEN ABOARD
A LITTLE LONGER.

LEO PROBST

THE LONGER I LIVE THE MORE BEAUTIFUL LIFE BECOMES.

Frank Lloyd Wright

DO A LITTLE

DANCE,

MAKE A

LITTLE LOVE

—

I'LL KEEP SWIVELLING MY HIPS UNTIL THEY NEED REPLACING.

—

TOM JONES

THERE'S A KIND OF
CONFIDENCE THAT
COMES WHEN YOU'RE IN
YOUR FORTIES AND FIFTIES,
AND MEN FIND THAT
INCREDIBLY **ATTRACTIVE**.

Peggy Northrop

I MUST BE CAREFUL
NOT TO GET TRAPPED
IN THE PAST. THAT'S
WHY I TEND TO
FORGET MY SONGS.

Mick Jagger

THE OLDER
ONE GROWS,

THE MORE
ONE LIKES
INDECENCY.

Virginia Woolf

I AM NOT OLD BUT MELLOW LIKE GOOD WINE.

Stephen Phillips

**THE ONLY
FORM OF EXERCISE
I TAKE IS MASSAGE.**

Truman Capote

WHEN OUR
VICES DESERT US,
WE FLATTER OURSELVES
THAT WE ARE DESERTING
OUR VICES.

FRANCOIS DE LA ROCHEFOUCAULD

IT'S SEX, NOT
YOUTH, THAT'S
WASTED ON
THE YOUNG.

Janet Harris

I'M LIMITLESS
AS FAR AS AGE IS
CONCERNED...

AS LONG AS HE HAS A
DRIVER'S LICENCE.

Kim Cattrall on dating younger men

IF YOU THINK HITTING 40 IS LIBERATING, WAIT TILL YOU HIT 50.

MICHELLE PFEIFFER

—

THE ANSWER TO OLD
AGE IS TO KEEP ONE'S
MIND BUSY AND TO
GO ON WITH ONE'S
LIFE AS IF IT WERE
INTERMINABLE.

—

LEON EDEL

WHEN CHOOSING
BETWEEN TWO EVILS,
I ALWAYS LIKE TO TRY
THE ONE I'VE NEVER
TRIED BEFORE.

Mae West

I AM GETTING TO AN AGE
WHEN I CAN ONLY ENJOY
THE LAST SPORT LEFT. IT
IS CALLED HUNTING FOR
YOUR SPECTACLES.

Edward Grey

YOUNG AT HEART

**MEN CHASE
GOLF BALLS WHEN
THEY'RE TOO OLD TO
CHASE ANYTHING ELSE.**

Groucho Marx

I'D RATHER BE DEAD
THAN SINGING
'SATISFACTION'
WHEN I'M 45.

Mick Jagger

I HAVE THE BODY OF AN
18-YEAR-OLD. I KEEP IT
IN THE FRIDGE.

SPIKE MILLIGAN

WE'RE NOT THE MEN OUR FATHERS WERE.

**IF WE WERE
WE WOULD BE
TERRIBLY OLD.**

Flann O'Brien

—

THE BEST YEARS OF A
WOMAN'S LIFE - THE
TEN YEARS BETWEEN
39 AND 40.

—

ANONYMOUS

YOU KNOW YOU ARE GETTING OLDER WHEN 'HAPPY HOUR' IS A NAP.

Gray Kristofferson

THE OLDER
I GET,
THE OLDER
OLD IS.

Tom Baker

BY THE TIME I HAVE
MONEY TO BURN, MY FIRE
WILL HAVE BURNT OUT.

Anonymous

GRANNY SAID SHE
WAS GOING TO GROW
OLD GRACEFULLY,

BUT SHE LEFT
IT TOO LATE.

Christine Kelly

IF YOU OBEY

ALL THE

RULES,

YOU MISS

ALL THE FUN.

KATHARINE HEPBURN

SOME KIDS
IN ITALY CALL
ME 'MAMA JAZZ';
I THOUGHT THAT
WAS SO CUTE. AS
LONG AS THEY
DON'T CALL ME
'GRANDMA JAZZ'.

Ella Fitzgerald

SOMETIMES WHEN
A MAN RECALLS THE
GOOD OLD DAYS, HE'S
REALLY THINKING OF
HIS BAD YOUNG DAYS.

ANONYMOUS

I DON'T PLAN
TO GROW OLD
GRACEFULLY;
I PLAN TO HAVE
FACELIFTS UNTIL
MY EARS MEET.

Rita Rudner

YOU'LL FIND
AS YOU GROW
OLDER THAT
YOU WEREN'T
BORN SUCH
A GREAT
WHILE AGO
AFTER ALL.

THE TIME
SHORTENS UP.

Frank Lloyd Wright

OLDER AND

WISER?

—

KEEP TRUE TO THE
DREAMS OF THY YOUTH.

—

FRIEDRICH VON SCHILLER

NONE ARE SO OLD AS THOSE WHO HAVE OUTLIVED ENTHUSIASM.

Henry David Thoreau

YOU'RE ONLY AS YOUNG
AS THE LAST TIME YOU
CHANGED YOUR MIND.

Timothy Leary

OLD AGE IS LIKE A PLANE FLYING THROUGH A STORM.

ONCE YOU ARE ABOARD
THERE IS NOTHING
YOU CAN DO.

Golda Meir

**IF YOU WANT
A THING DONE WELL,
GET A COUPLE OF OLD
BROADS TO DO IT.**

Bette Davis

A PRUNE IS AN EXPERIENCED PLUM.

John Trattner

FROM 40 TO 50 A MAN
MUST MOVE UPWARD, OR
THE NATURAL FALLING
OFF IN THE VIGOUR OF
LIFE WILL CARRY HIM
RAPIDLY DOWNWARD.

OLIVER WENDELL HOLMES JR

A MAN IS NOT OLD AS LONG AS HE IS SEEKING SOMETHING.

Jean Rostand

WISDOM DOESN'T NECESSARILY COME WITH AGE.

SOMETIMES AGE JUST SHOWS UP ALL BY ITSELF.

Tom Wilson

—

CHERISH ALL YOUR
HAPPY MOMENTS:
THEY MAKE A FINE
CUSHION FOR
OLD AGE.

—

CHRISTOPHER MORLEY

AS WE GROW OLDER,
OUR BODIES
GET SHORTER
AND OUR
ANECDOTES
LONGER.

ROBERT QUILLEN

LIVE, LOVE AND LAST

TO STOP AGEING,
KEEP ON RAGING.

Michael Forbes

EVERYONE IS THE AGE

OF THEIR HEART.

Guatemalan proverb

ONE SHOULD
NEVER MAKE ONE'S
DEBUT IN A SCANDAL.
ONE SHOULD RESERVE
THAT TO GIVE INTEREST
TO ONE'S OLD AGE.

Oscar Wilde

AT MIDDLE AGE THE
SOUL SHOULD BE
OPENING UP LIKE A
ROSE, NOT CLOSING
UP LIKE A CABBAGE.

John Andrew Holmes

AGE IS WHATEVER YOU THINK IT IS.

YOU ARE AS OLD AS YOU THINK YOU ARE.

Muhammad Ali

HE WHO LAUGHS, LASTS!

Mary Pettibone Poole

NO MATTER HOW
OLD YOU ARE,
THERE'S ALWAYS
SOMETHING GOOD TO
LOOK FORWARD TO.

LYNN JOHNSTON

—

AT AGE 20, WE WORRY ABOUT WHAT OTHERS THINK OF US. AT 40, WE DON'T CARE WHAT THEY THINK OF US.

—

ANN LANDERS

AGE DOES NOT PROTECT YOU FROM LOVE.

BUT LOVE, TO SOME EXTENT, PROTECTS YOU FROM AGE.

Jeanne Moreau

DON'T LET AGEING GET YOU DOWN.

IT'S TOO HARD
TO GET BACK UP.

John Wagner

TOMORROW'S
GONE –
WE'LL HAVE
TONIGHT!

Dorothy Parker

THERE ARE THREE STAGES
OF A MAN'S LIFE:
HE BELIEVES IN SANTA
CLAUS, HE DOESN'T
BELIEVE IN SANTA CLAUS,
HE IS SANTA CLAUS.

Anonymous

IT'S A GOOD IDEA TO OBEY ALL THE RULES WHEN YOU'RE YOUNG JUST SO YOU'LL HAVE THE STRENGTH TO BREAK THEM WHEN YOU'RE OLD.

Mark Twain

ILLS, PILLS AND TWINGES

MY DOCTOR TOLD ME
TO DO SOMETHING THAT
PUTS ME OUT OF BREATH,
SO I'VE TAKEN UP
SMOKING AGAIN.

JO BRAND

MIDDLE AGE IS

WHEN YOU CHOOSE YOUR CEREAL FOR THE FIBRE,

NOT THE TOY.

ANONYMOUS

I KEEP FIT. EVERY
MORNING I DO A
HUNDRED LAPS OF
AN OLYMPIC-SIZED
SWIMMING POOL IN A
SMALL MOTOR LAUNCH.

PETER COOK

I DON'T
WANT A FLU JAB.
I LIKE GETTING
FLU. IT GIVES ME
SOMETHING ELSE
TO COMPLAIN
ABOUT.

David Letterman

I'D LIKE TO LEARN TO SKI BUT I'M WORRIED ABOUT MY KNEES. THEY CREAK...

AND I'M AFRAID THEY MIGHT START AN AVALANCHE.

Jonathan Ross

AGE SELDOM ARRIVES
SMOOTHLY OR QUICKLY.
IT'S MORE OFTEN A
SUCCESSION OF JERKS.

Jean Rhys

NOTHING IS MORE RESPONSIBLE FOR THE GOOD OLD DAYS THAN A BAD MEMORY.

Franklin Pierce Adams

I GO SLOWER AS TIME GOES FASTER.

Mason Cooley

OLD MINDS ARE LIKE OLD HORSES; YOU MUST EXERCISE THEM IF YOU WISH TO KEEP THEM IN WORKING ORDER.

John Quincy Adams

WHAT MOST PERSONS CONSIDER AS VIRTUE,

AFTER THE AGE OF 40 IS SIMPLY A LOSS OF ENERGY.

Voltaire

I HOPE TO HAVE IT REPLACED VERY SOON.

Terry Wogan on people saying that he didn't know the meaning of 'hip'

LIFE IS A
MODERATELY GOOD
PLAY WITH A BADLY
WRITTEN THIRD ACT.

TRUMAN CAPOTE

I DON'T KNOW HOW YOU FEEL ABOUT OLD AGE... BUT IN MY CASE I DIDN'T EVEN SEE IT COMING. IT HIT ME FROM THE REAR.

PHYLLIS DILLER

CHIN UP,
CHEST
OUT

INFLATION IS WHEN
YOU PAY 15 DOLLARS
FOR THE 10-DOLLAR
HAIRCUT YOU USED TO
GET FOR 5 DOLLARS WHEN
YOU HAD HAIR.

Sam Ewing

WRINKLES ARE HEREDITARY.

PARENTS GET THEM FROM THEIR CHILDREN.

DORIS DAY

AS THE
ARTERIES
GROW HARD,

THE HEART
GROWS SOFT.

H. L. Mencken

AS WE GROW OLD...
THE BEAUTY
STEALS INWARD.

Ralph Waldo Emerson

I'M NOT DENYING MY AGE, I'M EMBELLISHING MY YOUTH.

Tamara Reynolds

THE SECRET OF
STAYING YOUNG IS
TO LIVE HONESTLY,
EAT SLOWLY AND LIE
ABOUT YOUR AGE.

Lucille Ball

THE EASIEST WAY
TO DIMINISH THE
APPEARANCE OF
WRINKLES IS TO KEEP
YOUR GLASSES OFF
WHEN YOU LOOK
IN THE MIRROR.

JOAN RIVERS

PEOPLE SAY THAT AGE IS JUST A STATE OF MIND.

I SAY IT'S MORE ABOUT THE STATE OF YOUR BODY.

Geoffrey Parfitt

PROFESSIONALLY, I HAVE NO AGE.

Kathleen Turner

—

YOU KNOW YOU'RE GETTING OLD WHEN YOU CAN PINCH AN INCH ON YOUR FOREHEAD.

—

JOHN MENDOZA

AS YOU GET OLDER, THE
PICKINGS GET SLIMMER,
BUT THE PEOPLE DON'T.

Carrie Fisher

WRINKLES SHOULD
MERELY INDICATE
WHERE SMILES
HAVE BEEN.

Mark Twain

If you're interested in finding out more
about our books, find us on Facebook
at **Summersdale Publishers**
and follow us on Twitter at
@Summersdale.

www.summersdale.com